POETICA 21
Slow Chrysanthemums

# Slow Chrysanthemums

CLASSICAL KOREAN POEMS
IN CHINESE

translated and introduced by
KIM JONG-GIL

Anvil Press Poetry

Published in 1987
by Anvil Press Poetry Ltd
69 King George Street London SE10 8PX
and 27 South Main Street Wolfeboro NH 03894

Copyright © Chi-gyu Kim 1987

This book is published with
financial assistance from
The Arts Council of Great Britain

Typeset in Horley Old Style
by Bryan Williamson, Swinton, Berwickshire
Chinese text set by Yeyong, Seoul
Printed and bound in England at
The Camelot Press plc, Southampton

*British Library Cataloguing in Publication Data*

Slow chrysanthemums : classical Korean poems
 in Chinese.
1. Chinese poetry – Korean authors  2. Chinese
poetry – Translations into English  3. English
poetry – Translations from Chinese
895.1'1'00809519   PL2518

*Library of Congress Cataloging-in-Publication Data*

Slow chrysanthemums.

 (Poetica; 21)
 Translated from Chinese.
  1. English poetry – Translations from Chinese.
2. Chinese poetry – Korean authors – Translations into
English.  I. Jong-gil, Kim, 1926-  .  II. Series.
PL3074.5.E5S56   1986   895.1'1   86-3506

ISBN 0-85646-162-8
ISBN 0-85646-163-6 (pbk.)

IN AFFECTIONATE MEMORY OF
SIR WILLIAM EMPSON

# Contents

| | | |
|---|---|---|
| Preface | | 11 |
| Introduction | | 13 |
| Ch'oe Ch'i-wǒn | On a Rainy Autumn Night | 25 |
| | At My Study in Mount Kaya | 26 |
| Ch'oe Kwang-yu | On a Spring Day in Chang-an | 27 |
| Chang Yǒn-u | Song of the Cold Pine Pavilion | 28 |
| Chǒng Chi-sang | The Taedong River | 29 |
| Kim Pu-shik | At the Kamno-sa Temple | 30 |
| Ko Cho-ki | At an Inn in Kŭmyang-hyǒn | 31 |
| Yi Il-lo | Written on the Wall of a Monastery | 32 |
| | Night Rain on the River Hsiao-hsiang | 33 |
| Im Ch'un | Travelling on a Winter Day | 34 |
| Yi Kyu-bo | The Moon in the Well | 35 |
| | To My Son Editing My Poems | 36 |
| | Along the Upper Reaches of the Nakdong River | 37 |
| Ch'oe Hang | Quatrain | 38 |
| Chin Hwa | Walking in the Field | 39 |
| Kim Kŭk-ki | An Old Fisherman | 40 |
| | At a Station House | 41 |
| Wǒngam | Written at Leisure | 42 |
| Yi Che-hyǒn | After the Snow in the Mountains | 43 |
| | A Love Song | 44 |
| Yi Kok | To a Friend | 45 |
| Yi Saek | Written on a Volume by a Friend | 46 |
| Chǒng Mong-ju | To My Husband at the Front | 47 |
| Chǒng To-jǒn | Visiting a Friend | 48 |
| | Visiting a Friend's Cottage | 49 |
| Yi Sung-in | A Monk's Hut | 50 |
| Kwǒn Kŭn | On a Spring Day in the South of the City | 51 |
| Kil Chae | My Intention | 52 |
| Sǒng Sam-mun | At the Execution Ground | 53 |
| Sǒ Kǒ-jǒng | Slow Chrysanthemums | 54 |
| Sǒng Kan | A Fisherman | 55 |
| Kim Shi-sŭp | Now Shine, Now Rain | 56 |

| | | |
|---|---|---|
| Tanjong | Hearing a Nightingale | 57 |
| Kim Koeng-p'il | My Way | 58 |
| Kim An-guk | On a Journey | 59 |
| Yi Haeng | Written on the Wall of an Office | 60 |
| Pak Ŏn | Thinking of a Friend | 61 |
| Yi Ŏn-jŏk | Doing Nothing | 62 |
| Im Ŏk-nyŏng | To a Friend | 63 |
| Yi Hwang | On a Pond in Spring | 64 |
| | On Horseback | 65 |
| Shin Saim-dang | Looking Homeward from a Mountain Pass | 66 |
| Hwang Chin-i | Meeting in Dreams | 67 |
| | Parting from a Lover | 68 |
| Hyu-jŏng | Climbing a Mountain Peak | 69 |
| Song Ik-p'il | Boating at Dusk | 70 |
| | To the Moon | 71 |
| Sŏng Hon | An Incidental Poem | 72 |
| Yi I | On Resigning Office | 73 |
| Chŏng Ch'ŏl | An Autumn Night | 74 |
| | Night at a Cottage | 75 |
| Paek Kwang-hun | Spring at Yongmun | 76 |
| Yi Sun-shin | At Night on the Hansan Isle | 77 |
| Im Che | Parting without a Word | 78 |
| Chang Hyŏn-gwang | Coming Home after a War | 79 |
| Yu Mong-in | A Poor Woman | 80 |
| Hŏ Ch'o-hi | A Lady's Complaint | 81 |
| | A Poor Girl | 82 |
| Shin Hŭm | On a Monk's Poetry Scroll | 83 |
| Kwŏn P'il | At the Grave of Chŏng Ch'ŏl | 84 |
| Sŭng I-kyo | On an Autumn Night | 85 |
| Song Han-p'il | An Incidental Poem | 86 |
| Kim Yŏn-gwang | On an Autumn Night | 87 |
| Yi Ok-bong | Waiting for a Lover | 88 |
| | Sorrows of Separation | 89 |
| | To a Lover | 90 |
| Kwŏn Kap | At the Old Capital | 91 |
| Yi Shik | A New Swallow | 92 |
| Yun Sŏn-do | At My Study | 93 |
| Yun Hwŏn | To a Friend Retired in the Country | 94 |

| | | |
|---|---|---|
| Hŏ Kyŏng-yun | A Mountain Home | 95 |
| Kang Paek-nyŏn | On New Year's Eve | 96 |
| Song Shi-yŏl | Going Up to the Capital | 97 |
| Ch'oe Ki-nam | Elegy on Myself | 98 |
| Ŏm Ŭi-gil | Sitting at Night | 99 |
| Cho Shin-jun | A Lady's Complaint | 100 |
| Kwŏn Tae-un | Passing an Old Capital | 101 |
| Kang Se-hwang | In the Alley | 102 |
| Pak Chi-wŏn | Looking into the Mirror on New Year's Day | 103 |
| Kyewŏl | Parting from a Lover | 104 |
| Chŏng Yak-yong | Lamenting Poverty | 105 |
| | Laughing by Myself | 106 |
| Yi Yang-yŏn | A Dream | 107 |
| Kim Chŏng-hi | Written on a Cottage Wall | 108 |
| | On Hearing, in Exile, of the Death of My Wife | 109 |
| Chŏng Sang-gwan | Ch'usŏk | 110 |
| Yi Sang-jŏk | On the Roadside Monument | 111 |
| Kim Pyŏng-yŏn | At an Inn | 112 |
| | To an Ungenerous Host | 113 |
| Kang Wi | On My Way to Such'un | 114 |
| Yi Chong-wŏn | Lodging in the Capital | 115 |
| Chŏng Pong | The East Lake | 116 |
| Hwang O | The Swing | 117 |
| Nŭngun | Waiting for a Lover | 118 |
| Anonymous Woman | In a Boat | 119 |
| Yi Ki | Peach Blossom | 120 |
| Anonymous Woman | On a Great-Granddaughter's Death | 121 |
| Hyejŏng | Autumn Rain at a Remote Temple | 122 |
| Hwang Hyŏn | Hearing of a Disaster | 123 |
| | On Killing Myself | 124 |
| Notes | | 125 |

# Preface

THIS ANTHOLOGY of one hundred classical Korean poems in Chinese covers a period of over a thousand years from the late ninth century to the end of the first decade of the twentieth. The majority of the poets included are represented by only one poem each; a dozen poets by two; and only two poets by as many as three. Poets are arranged in the chronological order of the dates of their birth, but where those dates are uncertain or unknown, the arrangement is necessarily conjectural.

The project out of which this book has evolved began several years ago. The work has been extremely time-consuming, more especially as it has involved the maintenance of a precarious balance, a sort of tightrope-walking, between two shaky poles. I mean of course the challenge of translating from Chinese to English, both of which languages I have acquired only by study. Needless to say, the more difficult part of the venture has been to make readable English versions with a maximum of both linguistic and poetic fidelity to the originals. It has entailed an almost endless process of revising and testing the drafts on such native speakers of English as I have been able to consult.

In order to bring out more saliently the Korean character of this particular genre, I have chosen poems free from Chinese allusions, and in making my selection I have also been guided to a certain extent by their popularity in Korea. Classical Chinese in poetic forms is inherently concise and terse, often requiring in translation a change of the original syntax or a sacrifice of the original sense and imagery. So I have taken some liberties with the literal sense of the original at times for the sake of poetic accuracy or rhythmic balance in the translated version. I have also used compression in translating the titles of some poems, when they are so specific that it hardly seems necessary to render them literally.

In preparing this slim volume, I am indebted to a number of people for their help; but my special thanks are due to Prof. Yi Tong-hwan for his kind explanations of points in the originals I inquired into; to Dr Rob Wilson for his patient reading of my first drafts; and to the late Sir William Empson for his magnanimity in preparing a dozen sheets of invaluable comments and suggestions regarding the versions I showed him in July, 1983. It must have taken him many hours during that unusually hot spell in London nine months before his death. That, among other things, is why I dedicate this volume to his memory. And last but not least, I express my gratitude to the Korean Culture and Arts Foundation for its grant and encouragement which have enabled me finally to complete this long and delicate undertaking.

Cambridge
*April, 1985*

# Introduction

UNTIL THE EARLY days of this century, poetry-writing in classical Chinese was very much a part of the life of an educated Korean. Chinese versification was regarded as an important discipline for Korean students in former times, a discipline at once aesthetic and moral. They studied Confucian texts and histories and literary works of ancient China, and were also made to memorize masterpieces of Chinese poetry and prose. Of the poetic texts they learned, *Shi-ching* (the Confucian Anthology) and the representative works of T'ang poets were indeed indispensable. Not only did they have to memorize them; they were also made to compose in the same forms and on the same models they had learned by heart. The test of their attainment was often whether they could write decent verse in Chinese and a scholarly reputation could depend, almost exclusively, on the quality of one's writing in the Chinese medium and metres. Thus in Korea in past ages, most scholars were poets and most poets were scholars.

All this, however, does not mean that the Korean people had no language of their own. On the contrary, they had a native language distinct from Chinese in all its linguistic features, but no systematic means of writing it down. This is the reason why they adopted Chinese characters and why classical Chinese remained the primary written language in Korea for such a long period. So deep-rooted, indeed, was this foreign medium in Korean intellectual life that when *Hangŭl*, the phonetic Korean alphabet, was invented and promulgated in the mid-fifteenth century it was virtually ignored and even despised by Korean scholars. For them the new writing system was too simple and too easy to learn, and it took over four hundred years for *Hangŭl* to replace Chinese in official and general use. In the meantime, it was used mostly by the womenfolk of the upper class and by certain literati when they tried their hands at writing Korean-language verse and prose. It is indeed small wonder that, up to the beginning of this century, the quantity of Korean poetry written in Chinese overwhelmed that of Korean poetry in its native language.

Brought up as a child in a Confucian family of a traditionally most learned milieu in Korea, I still remember clearly how the older members of my family devoted their lives to the study of Chinese and Chinese-language Korean classics and how much they loved to read and write in classical Chinese. I often had a chance of watching them having a 'poetry gathering' with their friends and relatives, either at home or at a country 'pavilion'. At such a gathering, they used to agree first on a common subject and a common set of 'rhyme characters' before they went on composing in their heads. Some kept sitting cross-legged on the floor, gently swaying their bodies from side to side; some standing, their hands clasped at the back of their waists, looking at a far-away corner of the sky or mountains; and some loitering in the garden or by a stream, humming to weigh the sounds and senses of Chinese words and phrases. When the poems were completed, they were written down, by dictation, in beautiful calligraphy on a 'poetry scroll' and appreciated by being chanted one after another. Meanwhile comments would be made on the poems and suggestions proposed to improve them, and then the whole event would end up with food and drinks.

Such gatherings were by no means the only occasions for writing poems for Korean scholars in earlier times; they took, in fact, almost every opportunity to compose them. They often sent poems to their friends, who replied in turn with poems employing the same 'rhyme characters' used in the poems sent to them. They wrote a variety of occasional poems: commemorative, congratulatory, and elegiac in addition to those of ordinary kinds: lyrical, descriptive, reflective, and even satirical. The frequent casualness of the titles they used, such as 'Written on the Wall of a Monastery', 'Written at Leisure', and 'An Incidental Poem', attests the fact that their poems could be prompted by numerous passing moments of their life. They were, however, never published in their lifetime; they went around only in manuscripts and in copies. As in Elizabethan England, there was a notion of the 'vulgarity of print' among the Korean poets of old times: their works were printed only after their death, and even then only if of sufficient merit and if their descendants could afford to defray the expenses.

The first piece of Korean poetry that has been handed down is a little lyric from Koguryŏ, an ancient Korean kingdom, which once spanned the greater part of the Korean peninsula and Manchuria from 37 BC to 668 AD. According to old records, the song was sung by Yuri, the second king of Koguryŏ in the early first century, when he had been deserted by his favourite concubine.

> Flutter, flutter the orioles,
> Male and female, together.
> But O, I am alone:
> With whom shall I go home?

Another celebrated poem from Koguryŏ is one of historical and military interest. It is a poem written by General Ŭlchi Mundŏk as a stratagem, when the army of Emperor Yang of Sui invaded Korea in the early seventh century. Having lured the enemy forces into the outskirts of P'yŏngyang, the general, under the guise of surrender, sent the poem to Yu Chung-wen, a General of the Sui army.

> Your godlike plans plumbed the heavens,
> Your subtle reckoning spanned the earth.
> You have won the battle, and made your name:
> Then, why not be content and withdraw?

It was, however, in the late eighth century in the kingdom of Silla (53 BC – 918 AD) that Korean poetry in Chinese attained a high level. Ch'oe Ch'i-wŏn, the greatest poet of the kingdom, went to China in 868, passed the T'ang civil service examination and held a number of official posts in China. He also became well-known as a poet, his works being published in one of the T'ang anthologies. His poem 'On a Rainy Autumn Night' was presumably written in China, but another poem of his, 'At My Study in Mount Kaya', belongs to his later years when he was back in Korea and had retired to the mountain in the last years of Silla. His contemporary Ch'oe Kwang-yu also studied in China, and his poem 'On a Spring Day in Chang-an' reveals his homesickness and frustration during his study abroad. These poets, like most poets of later generations who wrote in Chinese, were Confucian scholars and officials. Ch'oe Ch'i-wŏn, however, set another precedent for a number of later poets by being at the same time deeply connected with Buddhism. Mount Kaya to which he retired in his later years is, in fact, the site of Haein-sa, one of the important Buddhist temples of the Silla period.

The subsequent kingdoms of the Koryŏ and Yi Dynasties also saw a great flowering of Chinese-language poetry. It was written not only by Confucian scholars and statesmen, but also by Buddhist monks and masters. During the Koryŏ period (918 – 1392), such a poet as Wŏngam was a Buddhist, and so was Ch'oe Hang for a time before he came into power in succession to his father, Ch'oe U. Some Confucian poets of the period also leaned conspicuously towards Buddhism: prominent among them were Kim Pu-shik, who was also a great historian, and Yi Il-lo, who was the first remarkable Korean critic as well as being an outstanding poet of the era. Even Yi Kyu-bo, a great man of letters and Confucian statesman of Koryŏ, has such a distinctly Buddhist poem as 'The Moon in the Well'. A similar poet was Yi Saek who served as an official in both Yüan and Koryŏ like his father, Yi Kok;

he almost became a Buddhist in his later years after the fall of the Koryŏ Dynasty. It is true that during the Koryŏ period Buddhism exerted a great influence on national life; but the Yi Dynasty (1392-1910) was predominantly Confucian. This great Confucian era, however, did not lack in Buddhist poets. Hyujŏng, the Great Master of Sŏsan, who led thousands of warrior-monks against the Japanese invasion towards the end of the sixteenth century, is perhaps the greatest among them. And again such a Confucian poet as Kim Shi-sŭp, who was one of King Tanjong's 'six loyal subjects who survived', in fact, lived as a Buddhist monk for many years.

A remarkable fact about the Yi Dynasty period is that it produced a number of talented women poets who wrote in Chinese. It is remarkable because, in those days when women were seldom given formal education, they educated themselves in Chinese and in its rigid versification. Some of them, such as Shin Saim-dang, the celebrated mother of the eminent scholar-official, Yi I, and Hŏ Ch'o-hi, better known by her pseudonym Nansŏl-hŏn, were formidable ladies from respected upper-class families; others, perhaps greater in number, were not. Hwang Chin-i is a typical case, being simply a *kisaeng*, the Korean counterpart of a Japanese *geisha*. It was, however, her low social status that allowed her to write poems explicitly concerned with love, a subject which was largely taboo for Confucian poets of the upper class. Such were Sŭng I-kyo, Yi Ok-bong, Kyewŏl and Nŭngun, as well as Hwang Chin-i, all of them being either *kisaengs* or concubines. Similarly, lower-class poets are also found among men of the period, such as Song Ik-p'il and So Han-p'il, Ch'oe Ki-nam and Chŏng Pong. The brothers Song Ik-p'il and Song Han-p'il were born of a mother who was a slave, and Chŏng Pong was once a servant in an upper-class household. And Kim Pyŏng-yŏn, usually known as Kim Satkat ('the big hat woven with bamboo-shreds'), came from a disgraced upper-class family and, deprived of the hope of a respectable career, made himself a tramp, often begging meals and improvising sarcastic poems.

These socially underprivileged poets, however, suffered no literary discrimination; their poetry, in fact, was loved and admired the more for their plight in society. So was, and indeed still is, the poetry of such poets as Chŏng Mong-ju, Sŏng Sam-mun, Yi Sun-shin and Hwang Hyŏn, but for different reasons. These are poets who have been particularly admired by the Korean nation, for they embraced causes dear to them at the cost of their lives. Chŏng Mong-ju, who was a great scholar-official towards the end of the Koryŏ Dynasty, refused, at the risk of his life, to cooperate with Yi Sŏng-gye, the founder of the Yi Dynasty, in order to remain loyal to his own dynasty. Sŏng Sam-mun, one of King Tanjong's 'six loyal subjects who died', was killed for his part in an attempt to restore the king who had been forced to abdicate his throne. Yi Sun-shin was a famous Korean admiral who invented the world's first iron-clad vessel; but he has been no less respected for his unselfish dedication to the defence of the country against the afore-mentioned Japanese invasion than for his superb naval tactics. And Hwang-Hyŏn was a distinguished poet and intransigent critic who killed himself in protest against Japan's annexation of Korea in 1910. Thus it is quite natural that, at least for Korean readers, the integrity of these poets should enhance the poignancy of their poetry.

As has been pointed out at the outset, almost all the educated in Korea were poets in those days; for them poetry was indeed a 'superior amusement', as T.S. Eliot once defined it, recording their actual experiences and expressing their real feelings. Traditionally in China and Korea, poetry was believed to be *yen-chi*, 'the utterance of what is in one's mind'. Thus it was usually of a highly personal kind, admitting almost no distinction between the poem and the poet. It was regarded as a direct expression of the poet's own self and, therefore, as the spontaneous reflection of feelings, sentiments and attitudes in his actual life. As has also been mentioned, it was an important personal discipline vital to the formation of one's character, as is suggested by Confucius's frequent and almost pragmatic reference to the use of poetry in his *Analects* and elsewhere. So deep-seated in the ancient Eastern mind was this belief in the proximity between poetry and its author that it was often thought to be prophetic of his own future destiny. This Eastern version of the Roman concept of the poet as *vates* gave rise to the notion that a poem, often a very clever one, could prove to be fatal to the poet himself. In Korea, such a poem used to be called a *tanmyŏngku*, literally a 'life-shortening poem', which young scholars were warned against writing. This and similar Confucian scruples, it seems, have been operative in determining the general temper of classical Eastern and Korean poetry.

For Western readers, Korean poetry in Chinese might not appear strikingly distinct from traditional Chinese poetry, just as the facial features of the Koreans, for them, are hardly distinguishable from those of the Chinese. It is, however, only natural that it should read like Chinese poetry, because it is in the same medium and forms and on roughly the same subjects. Its themes and sentiments are, of course, various: joys and sorrows; loneliness and nostalgia; self-mockery over one's vanity and misfortune; and even pathos in the face of one's own death. These themes and sentiments are almost invariably treated and expressed in and through natural backgrounds: mountains and valleys; streams and rivers; the moon, rain and wind; grass, trees and flowers. In consequence, the world embodied in it resembles the typical scene of a traditional Eastern painting with leisurely detached people occupying a small space in a corner or in the foreground of a landscape of misty mountains and rivers and lakes. Poetry, however, is not painting; thanks to its medium of language, it can reveal man's states of mind in the flux of time with greater explicitness and intelligibility. It also can play upon ideas and logic to an extent that no other art can possibly emulate in intellectual perspicuity. Whatever the setting and situation, therefore, a poem has its own specific human aspect based on its intellectual and emotional content. It is particularly in this human aspect of Korean poetry in Chinese that one may hope to come to grips with the elusive subject of its Koreanness.

It still remains very difficult, however, to draw a feasible distinction between traditional Chinese poetry and classical Korean poetry in the medium of Chinese. Almost all the themes and sentiments of the latter, for example, are found in the former almost exactly in the same manner. Hence such differences as there may be between the two very similar poetries are to be discovered not so much in their typical properties as in the degree to which such properties occur. Readers may notice at once the frequent appearance of mountains in Korean poetry in Chinese, while they will but rarely encounter in it the great rivers and expansive lakes which frequently appear in its Chinese counterpart. This difference, of course, derives from the geographical difference between China and Korea; and it is perhaps too obvious a feature to deserve dwelling upon. So let it suffice to consider here only one aspect of Korean poetry in Chinese which seems to characterize it in an important way. It is the marked propensity of the poets to withdrawal from the world, a propensity which often involves a kind of philosophical transcendence.

This tendency is by no means peculiar to the Korean poets, deriving partly from the prevalent instinct in traditional Eastern poets and philosophers, famously exemplified by T'ao Ch'ien (372-430) in his poem 'Words on Returning Home'. In classical Korean poetry, however, this tradition of withdrawal is especially prominent and has a specific historical significance as a reflection of the social conditions in which they found themselves. The world they lived in seems to have been, and indeed was, a turbulent one that made them constantly desire to transcend it. Their love of nature and of the leisurely life, their acquiescence in anonymity in 'clean poverty' and their scorn for vanity and worldly power, all derive from this same desire. It was their ideal to live in detachment from all the vulgarities and conflicts of the world by being as much assimilated with nature as possible. All this may seem to suggest a mere escapism or even defeatism; and it would be difficult to assert that it was entirely free from such things. But there was another more significant side to it which differentiated it from a mere retreat of the defeated. Korean Confucians, especially those neo-Confucians of the Yi Dynasty tended to be so austere in their principles that they were continually divided into tenacious factions on social, political, and even theoretical matters. Thus during the Yi Dynasty, in particular, Korean society was very factious, so much so that sensible scholars and poets had to try constantly to stand aloof from its wrangles. It was a significant token of their wisdom that they should choose to turn away from all the mess and muddle of the world.

Their fear of getting involved in violent social strife often achieves poetic transcendence primarily through robust and graceful irony. Even the seemingly straightforward 'fear' of 'disputes over right and wrong' in Ch'oe Ch'i-wŏn's poem, 'At My Study in Mount Kaya' (p.26), turns out to be not so simple as it might seem at first sight. In fact it contributes to an affirmation of his positive stance towards the world, because it is not so much the cause of his retiring from the world as the justification of his choice of the magnificent landscape where the mountain stream's 'frenzied rush through the rocks roars at the peaks'. It is this jaunty stance that justifies the almost presumptuous assumption on the part of the poet: 'I have arranged the waters to cage in these mountains.'

A similar kind of robust irony may be found in the poets of much later ages as well. Yun Sŏn-do, a great seventeenth-century poet who wrote in both Korean and Chinese, belonged to the faction of the 'Southern Men', largely out of power in the latter half of the Yi Dynasty. His poem 'At My Study' (p.93), in spite of its ostensible detachment and nonchalance, conceals a heart seething with political passion. He begins the poem with an apparent indifference to the world: 'My eyes fixed on the mountains and my ears on the lute, / How could affairs of the world ever disturb my mind?' This, again, is ironical, because the poet suggests that his proclaimed peace of mind is only apparent, and this in turn implies that there is something that causes him to struggle with himself. In reality, his mind is being very much disturbed by 'affairs of the world', though he pretends it is not. That is why he declares with deliberate buoyancy that 'Though nobody knows I am full of lively spirits, / Wildly I sing out a song, and then intone it alone.' Another poet of the same century, Song Shi-yŏl, who was a great scholar and also the leader of the faction called the 'Old Arguers', then in power, plays upon a similar irony in a different direction. His poem 'Going Up to the Capital' (p.97) shows a paradoxical reflection on the occasion of his going into politics and power. Even at the moment of excitement, the poet contemplates the reverse side of its significance, finding that even the waters and mountains hate his 'going into the wind and dust.'

This dialectic of paradoxical irony or of a double vision attains a remarkable elegance and subtlety in such later poets as Yi Sang-jŏk, Kim Pyŏng-yŏn and Kang Wi. Yi Sang-jŏk, a noted poet and calligrapher, who served as a local magistrate himself, has a satirical poem, 'On the Roadside Monument' (p.111). The subject of the poem is a monument erected to extol the former chief of a county who was, in fact, notorious for his avarice and cruelty while in office. It was an old and often hypocritical Korean custom to erect such a memorial stone in honour of a former local magistrate, a practice which provided his successor with a chance for further extortion and corruption. Thus in this poem, the poet speaks with his tongue in his cheek: 'The piece of stone is speechless at the roadside: / How can the new magistrate compare with the old?' What he really means by implication is, of course, that neither the old nor the new official is really entitled to such an honour. Kim Pyŏng-yŏn was, as has been mentioned, a tramp-poet, and his poem 'To an Ungenerous Host' (p.113) was prompted by his being treated humiliatingly at a house where he begged a meal. The meal of gruel he was given in the yard, not in the house, was so thin and watery that it reflected 'the sunlight and the wandering clouds'. But he pretends to be high-minded, and so he is in a sense when, telling the mean host not to be ashamed of himself, he adds: 'I love to see the mountains come imaged in water.'

This gallant feat of poetic simulation achieves, through a sardonic irony, a transcendence of his humiliation and personal misery. A similar dialectic is found in Kang Wi's poem 'On My Way to Such'un' (p.114), in which the poet laments his own destitution and appears to be indulging in self-pity when he says: 'Alas! I am poorer than the willows on the long river-bank.' But here again the poet rises elegantly above his misery and self-pity by comparing himself with the willows which have already shed their cotton-like catkins, changing their dress into a spring garment of green. It is through this paradoxical identification of the poet himself with the natural phenomenon that he is able to overcome his own situation. Such an intimate relationship between the poet and nature may readily be perceived even in the necessarily brief selection of poems that it has been possible to consider here. Of the total of six poems, five are related to nature in one way or another, and this in itself bespeaks the preponderance of nature in classical Korean poetry in Chinese and indeed in traditional Eastern poetry at large. It might well be called a 'nature poetry' as a whole, but in a quite different sense from that associated with the poetry of Wordsworth. Nature in traditional Chinese or Korean poetry is not so much a partner of the poet with whom he holds communion as the very ambience of his life and poetry. He is indeed one with nature; and, as we have seen, albeit briefly, he has been capable of overcoming his pains and miseries within but through it.

KIM JONG-GIL

# On a Rainy Autumn Night

Bitter comes my song in the autumn wind;
So few friends have I had in all my life.
Outside the window drips the midnight rain:
Under the lamplight, my thought drifts far away.

秋夜雨中

秋風惟苦吟
世路少知音
窓外三更雨
燈前萬里心

崔致遠

CH'OE CH'I WŎN   857-?

# At My Study in Mount Kaya

The frenzied rush through the rocks roars at the peaks
And drowns out the human words close at hand.
As I always fear disputes over right and wrong,
I have arranged the waters to cage in these mountains.

題伽倻山讀書堂

狂奔疊石吼重巒
人語難分咫尺間
常恐是非聲到耳
故教流水盡籠山

崔致遠

CH'OE CH'I WŎN

# On a Spring Day in Chang-an

I can't shake the street dust from my hemp clothes;
In the glass at dawn, my hair turns grey, my face withers.
The flowers here are gorgeous, though I am sad:
The trees of my old garden green in my dreams.
Oh to drift over the sea, homeward under the hazy moon;
With my poor horse, I'm sick of asking which ford to cross.
I failed to study hard by the light of fireflies and snow
And now am hurt even by orioles in green willows.

長安春日有感

麻衣難拂路歧塵
鬢改顏衰曉鏡新
上國好花愁裏艷
故園芳樹夢中春
扁舟烟月思浮海
羸馬關河倦問津
祇爲未酬螢雪志
綠楊鶯語大傷神

崔匡裕

CH'OE KWANG-YU  *ninth to tenth century*

## Song of the Cold Pine Pavilion

The moon stands white over Cold Pine Pavilion:
The autumn waves are calm on Mirror Lake.
Listen to the sad cry coming and going:
The friendly gulls from the sand by the sea.

寒松亭曲

月白寒松夜
波安鏡浦秋
哀鳴來又去
有信一沙鷗

張延祐

CHANG YŎN-U  ?–1015

# The Taedong River

After the rain, the grass is rich on the long river-bank:
Seeing you off at a ford, I burst into sorrowful song.
When will the water of the Taedong River be exhausted?
Year after year, tears of separation add to its green waves.

大同江

雨歇長堤草色多
送君南浦動悲歌
大同江水何時盡
別淚年年添綠波

鄭知常

CHŎNG CHI-SANG   ?–1135

# At the Kamno-sa Temple

To where the vulgar do not come
I have climbed and feel serene.
The mountains look better in autumn;
Even at night the river gleams.
The white birds fly up and are gone;
The sailing boat goes lightly, alone.
Half my life I've spent, to my shame,
In this small world coveting fame.

甘露寺次韻

俗客不到處
登臨意思清
山形秋更好
江色夜猶明
白鳥高飛盡
孤帆獨去輕
自慚蝸角上
半世覓功名

金富軾

KIM PU-SHIK    1075–1151

## At an Inn in Kŭmyang-hyŏn

Dawn birds twitter in the frosty forest;
Wind breaks the traveller's sleep.
The crescent lingers over the eaves,
And I alone at an edge of the sky.
Fallen leaves hide my path home:
Last night's smoke hangs on the cold boughs.
My home still lies far to the west of the river,
And in this river-side village, autumn expires.

宿金壤縣

鳥語霜林曉
風驚客榻眠
簷殘半規月
人在一涯天
落葉埋歸路
寒枝掛宿煙
江東行未盡
秋盡水村邊

高兆基

KO CHO-KI　?–1157

# Written on the Wall of a Monastery

I waited for a friend, but he didn't come,
I looked for a monk, but he wasn't there.
Only a bird from beyond the forest
Cordially invited me for a drink.

書天壽僧院壁

待客客未到
尋僧僧亦無
唯餘林外鳥
款曲勸提壺

李仁老

YI IL-LO    1152–1220

# Night Rain on the River Hsiao-hsiang

A stretch of blue water between the shores in autumn:
The wind sweeps light rain over a boat coming back.
As the boat is moored at night near the bamboos,
Each leaf rustles coldly, awakening sorrow.

瀟湘夜雨

一帶蒼波兩岸秋
風吹細雨灑歸舟
夜來泊近江邊竹
葉葉寒聲總是愁

李仁老

YI IL-LO

# Travelling on a Winter Day

How many station houses have I passed by,
Since I left Nakchu alone at dawn?
I came on horseback through flurries of white snow,
Counting, with my whip, the jumbled blue mountains.
The moon set beyond the sky, warning me to return;
The wind blew cold in the field, sobering my drunken face.
I wanted to stop overnight in a remote village,
But the gate had closed early at every house.

冬日途中

凌晨獨出洛州城
幾許長亭與短亭
跨馬行衝微雪白
擧鞭吟數亂峯青
天邊日落歸心促
野外風寒醉面醒
寂寞孤村投宿處
人家門戶早常扃

林　椿

IM CH'UN   *later twelfth century*

# The Moon in the Well

A monk coveted the moon in the well
And fished it up with water into a bottle.
But back at the temple, he will find
When the bottle tilts, the moon spills.

詠井中月

山僧貪月色
并汲一瓶中
到寺方應覺
瓶傾月亦空

李奎報

YI KYU-BO    1168–1241

# To My Son Editing My Poems

I have always feared withering sooner than grass and trees,
But I find the volumes of my poor poems worse than
    nothing.
Who will know, a thousand years from now,
That a man named Yi was born in a corner of Korea?




兒子涵編詩文書其後

常恐身先草木枯
區區詩卷不如無
茫然千載還知否
姓李人生東海隅

李奎報

YI KYU-BO

# Along the Upper Reaches of the Nakdong River

By the path winding through the mountains,
I stroll at leisure along the Nakdong River.
Deep is the grass sprinkled with dew:
The pines are quiet; there is no wind.
The autumn waters as green as a duck's head,
The morning mist as red as a monkey's blood.
Nobody knows that this idle traveller
Is an old poet of world-wide fame.


過洛東江上流

百轉青山裏
閒行過洛東
草深猶有露
松靜自無風
秋水鴨頭綠
曉霞猩血紅
誰知倦遊客
四海一詩翁

李奎報

YI KYU-BO

# Quatrain

The moon in my garden is a smokeless candle;
The reflection of hills in my room, a voluntary guest;
The pine trees improvise on their strings the unscored
    tunes:
I enjoy them alone, having no one to share them with.

絶　句

滿庭月色無烟燭
入座山光不速賓
更有松絃彈譜外
只堪珍重未傳人

崔　沆

CH'OE HANG　?–1257

# Walking in the Field

Plum blossoms have fallen, the willows droop;
I pace up and down slowly in the mountain breeze.
Whispers are heard from the closed fisherman's house
And over the river pass the green threads of rain.

野　步

小梅零落柳㒈垂
閑踏青嵐步步遲
漁店閉門人語少
一江春雨碧絲絲

陳　澕

CHIN HWA　　*twelfth to thirteenth century*

# An Old Fisherman

Heaven has never been generous to the old fisherman
And seldom sent fair weather to the rivers and lakes.
Do not, old fisher, laugh at the rough human world:
You have chosen to put yourself amidst eddies and rapids.

漁　翁

天翁尚未貰漁翁
故遣江湖少順風
人生嶮巇君莫笑
自家還在急流中

金克己

KIM KŬK-KI　　*twelfth to thirteenth century*

## At a Station House

Though nearing fifty years in the life-span of man,
Little luck have I had in my ill-fated career.
What have I achieved during the years away from home?
I have come back empty-handed from so far away.
Still the forest birds warble kindly to me;
The wild flowers, wordless, smile to make me stay.
So the devil of poetry nags at me everywhere:
Together with poverty, that is my trouble's cause.

高原驛

百歲浮生逼五旬
奇區世路少通津
三年去國成何事
萬里歸家只此身
林鳥有情啼向客
野花無語笑留人
詩魔觸處來相惱
不待窮愁已苦辛

金克己

KIM KŬK-KI

# Written at Leisure

I raise the screen to let in the hue of hills
And connect a duct, dividing the stream's sound.
Few have come here all through the morning;
There is only a cuckoo calling his own name.

閑中雜詠(其一)

捲箔引山色
連筒分澗聲
終朝少人到
杜宇自呼名

釋圓鑑

WŎNGAM 1226–1292

## After the Snow in the Mountains

The paper quilt grows cold, the temple light dim;
The novice has not rung a bell all through the night.
He will start grumbling if I open the door so early,
But I have to see the garden pine laden with snow.

山中雪後

紙被生寒佛燈暗
沙彌一夜不鳴鍾
應嗔宿客開門早
要看庭前雪壓松

李齊賢

YI CHE-HYŎN   1287–1367

# A Love Song

Under the willow by the stream where I rinsed my silk,
I whispered to the young gallant, clasping his hand.
The rain has dropped from the eaves for three months;
How can I wash my finger-tips where his scent remains?

濟危寶

浣紗溪上傍垂楊
執手論心白馬郎
縱有連簷三月雨
指頭何忍洗餘香

李齊賢

YI CHE-HYŎN

## To a Friend

On a small boat, my life-long wish unattained,
I come home, hair already white, laughing at myself.
Still I dream of service at the Emperor's court
And forget that I am now among flowering reeds.

寄鄭代言

百年心事一扁舟
自笑歸來已白頭
猶有皇朝玉堂夢
不知身在荻花洲

李　穀

YI KOK　　1298–1351

# Written on a Volume by a Friend

The path runs aslant, deep among confused mountains;
At sundown, cattle find their way home on their own.
This is indeed the wish of an old man come true:
The sweet grass, faintly misted, reaches to the sky.

題牧菴卷

亂山深處路橫斜
日暮牛羊自識家
此是老翁真境界
淡煙芳草接天涯

李 穡

YI SAEK    1328–1396

# To My Husband at the Front

As I have hardly heard from you in years,
I cannot be sure if you are alive at the front.
This morning, I send you some clothes against the cold,
And the boy who was in my womb when I saw you off
    in tears

征婦怨

一別年多消息稀
塞垣存没有誰知
今朝始寄寒衣去
泣送歸時在腹兒

鄭夢周

CHŎNG MONG-JU    1337–1392

# Visiting a Friend

Smoke, dim and faint, silhouettes the trees high and low;
Grass covers up the track, so one is likely to stray.
As I am still lost, though nearing your house,
An old farmer, without turning, points west of a bridge.

訪金益之

墟烟暗淡樹高低
草沒人蹤路欲迷
行近君家猶未識
田翁背指小橋西

鄭道傳

CHŎNG TO-JŎN  1337–1398

# Visiting a Friend's Cottage

Autumn clouds are dreary over the hushed mountains;
Falling leaves, soundless, crimson the ground.
I stopped my horse by a bridge to ask my way,
Unaware that I stood in the scene of a painting.

訪金居士野居

秋陰漠漠四山空
落葉無聲滿地紅
立馬溪橋問歸路
不知身在畫圖中

鄭道傳

CHŎNG TO-JŎN

# A Monk's Hut

Where a track diverges north and south of the mountain,
Pine-pollen, soaked with rain, scatters.
The monk returns to his hut with water from a spring,
And a stretch of blue smoke colours the white cloud.

題僧舍

山南山北細路分
松花含雨落繽紛
道人汲井歸茅舍
一帶青煙染白雲

李崇仁

YI SUNG-IN   1349–1392

# On a Spring Day in the South of the City

Suddenly a spring breeze announces the season;
The fine rain still drizzles at day's end.
Apricot blossoms begin to burst at a house-corner,
Some of its dew-wet branches bend towards me.

春日城南即事

春風忽已近清明
細雨霏霏晚未晴
屋角杏花開欲遍
數枝含露向人傾

權　近

KWŎN KŬN　　1352–1409

## My Intention

Living alone under the thatched roof by a stream,
I am full of joy with the white moon and the fresh wind.
No guest comes, but the mountain birds are twittering;
I place my bed among the bamboos, lie down and read.

述　志

臨溪茅屋獨閒居
月白風清興有餘
外客不來山鳥語
移床竹塢臥看書

吉　再

KIL CHAE　　1358–1419

# At the Execution Ground

The beating drum presses for my life;
I turn and see the sun is about to set.
No inn is provided by the nether world;
At whose house will I sleep tonight?

受刑時作

擊鼓催人命
回頭日欲斜
黃泉無一店
今夜宿誰家

成三問

SŎNG SAM-MUN    1418–1456

## Slow Chrysanthemums

The chrysanthemums are slow to bloom this year,
I have not found autumn joy by the eastern hedge.
Heartless, indeed, is the west wind: it blows
Into my greying hair, not the yellow chrysanthemums.

菊花不開悵然有作

佳菊今年開較遲
一秋清興謾東籬
西風大是無情思
不入黃花入鬢絲

徐居正

SŎ KŎ-JŎNG   1420–1488

# A Fisherman

Mountains rise over mountains and smoke from valleys;
The dust of the world can never touch the white gulls.
The old fisherman is by no means disinterested:
In his boat, he owns the moon over the west river.

漁 父

數疊青山數谷烟
紅塵不到白鷗邊
漁翁不是無心者
管領西江月一船

成 侃

SŎNG KAN　　1427–1456

## Now Shine, Now Rain

Now shine, now rain, and rain becomes shine:
That is the skies' way, as well as men's.
My glory may well lead to my ruin;
Your escape from fame will bring you a name.
Flowers may open or fall, but spring doesn't care;
Clouds will come and go, but mountains do not argue.
I tell you, men of the world, you must remember
Nowhere will you find happiness all your life.

乍晴乍雨

乍晴乍雨雨還晴
天道猶然況世情
譽我便是足毀我
逃名却自爲求名
花開花謝春何管
雲去雲來山不爭
寄語世人須記認
取歡無處得平生

金時習

KIM SHI-SŬP    1435–1493

## Hearing a Nightingale

Since I left the imperial palace like a resentful bird,
I have dragged my lonely shadow among the blue
　　mountains.
I ask for sleep night after night, but sleep won't come,
Year after year passes in grief, but grief doesn't end.
Singing stopped, the moon is pale over the peaks at dawn;
Blood streamed, fallen petals are red in spring valleys.
When heaven is deaf to the song of a nightingale,
Why are a grieving man's ears so susceptible?


聞子規

一自冤禽出帝宮
孤身隻影碧山中
假眠夜夜眠無假
窮恨年年恨不窮
聲斷曉岑殘月白
血流春谷落花紅
天聾尚未聞哀訴
何奈愁人耳獨聰

端　宗

TANJONG　　1441–1457

# My Way

I live in peace and quiet, confining myself to home;
Only the moon is invited to shine on my loneliness.
Please do not ask me how I am getting along:
There are endless misty waves and hills on hills.

書　懷

處獨居閒絕往還
只呼明月照孤寒
憑君莫問生涯事
萬頃烟波數疊山

金宏弼

KIM KOENG-P'IL　　1454–1504

# On a Journey

At an edge of the sky, I grieve over my youth;
I long for home, but home is still far away.
As spring lets loose the wayward east wind,
A wild peach, unowned, opens its blossoms.

途中即事

天涯遊子惜年華
千里思歸未到家
一路東風春不管
野桃無主自開花

金安國

KIM AN-GUK    1478–1534

# Written on the Wall of an Office

Illness may strike me, busy in my declining years;
Spring can hardly stir me to write poetry.
Waking from a nap, I am surprised to find
Flowers fading and the roses wet with rain.

書直舍壁

衰年奔走病如期
春興無多不到詩
睡起忽驚花事晚
一番微雨濕薔薇

李　荇

YI HAENG　　1478-1534

# Thinking of a Friend

Snow melts and swells the stream,
Crows fly towards the clouds at dusk.
Sobered by the scene from drunkenness,
I write a new poem and again think of you.

萬　里

雪添春澗水
烏趁暮山雲
清境渾醒醉
新詩更憶君

朴　誾

PAK ŬN　　1479–1504

# Doing Nothing

All things change and keep no fixed state,
I adapt myself at leisure to flowing time.
As my strength has declined in recent years,
I look long at mountains, but do not write poems.

無 爲

萬物變遷無定態
一身閑適自隨時
年來漸省經營力
長對青山不賦詩

李彥迪

YI ŎN-JŎK   1491–1553

# To a Friend

At the gate of an old temple, another spring ends,
Sprinkling my clothes with petals and rain.
As I return, sleeves full of the sweet fragrance,
Mountain bees swarm after me from afar.

示子芳

古寺門前又送春
殘花隨雨點衣頻
歸來滿袖清香在
無數山蜂遠趁人

林億齡

IM ŎK-NYŎNG    1496–1568

## On a Pond in Spring

The dewy grass softly, softly encloses the water
Of a small pond, fresh and clean without a speck.
The pond is meant to mirror flying clouds and birds,
But I fear that swallows at times break its surface.

游春詠野塘

露草夭夭繞水涯
小塘清活淨無沙
雲飛鳥過元相管
只怕時時燕蹴波

李　滉

YI HWANG　　1501–1570

# On Horseback

Going out in the morning, I stoop to hear the stream;
Returning at dusk, I look up at the blue mountains.
Thus I spend mornings and evenings with mountains
    and waters,
Mountains like blue screens and waters like clear mirrors.
In the mountains, I wish to dwell as a crane in the clouds,
By the waters, to drift as a gull over the waves.
Wondering if official service hasn't wrecked my life,
I make bold to boast that I linger in a spirit land.

馬　上

朝行俯聽清溪響
暮歸遠望青山影
朝行暮歸山水中
山如蒼屏水明鏡
在山願爲棲雲鶴
在水願爲游波鷗
不知符竹誤我事
強顏自謂遊丹丘

李　滉

YI HWANG

## Looking Homeward from a Mountain Pass

Leaving my old mother in the seaside town,
Alas! I am going alone up to Seoul.
As I turn, once in a while, to look homeward on my way,
White clouds rush down the darkening blue mountains.

踰大關嶺望親庭

慈親鶴髮在臨瀛
身向長安獨去情
回首北坪時一望
白雲飛下暮山青

申師任堂

SHIN SAIM-DANG    1504–1552

# Meeting in Dreams

My wish to see you is fulfilled only in dreams;
Whenever I visit my joy, you visit me.
So let us dream again some future night,
Starting at the same time to meet on our way.

詠　夢

相思相見只憑夢
儂訪歡時歡訪儂
願使遙遙他夜夢
一時同作路中逢

黃眞伊

HWANG CHIN-I    c.1506–1544

## Parting from a Lover

The paulownia in the garden sheds its leaves under the moon;
Wild chrysanthemums yellow and wither in the frost.
In the pavilion that soars into the sky
We have got drunk over many a cup of wine.
Coldly the stream mingles with the sound of my lyre;
Sweetly the 'plum blossoms' drift through your flute.
We part in the morning, but my love will ever be
With you, my lord, over the far blue waves.

奉別蘇判書世讓

月下庭梧盡
霜中野菊黃
樓高天一尺
人醉酒千觴
流水和琴冷
梅花入笛香
明朝相別後
情與碧波長

黃眞伊

HWANG CHIN-I

# Climbing a Mountain Peak

The myriad cities look as small as ant-hills;
The brave by the thousand, maggots in a meat sauce.
Pillowed in serenity, as the moon catches a window,
I hear the wind-tossed pines rustling irregular rhymes.

登香爐峯

萬國都城如蟻垤
千家豪傑若醯雞
一窓明月清虛枕
無限松風韻不齊

釋休靜

HYU-JŎNG   1520-1604

# Boating at Dusk

Lost among flowers, the boat returns late;
Expecting the moon, it drifts slowly down the shoals.
Though I am drunk, I still drop a line:
The boat moves on, but not my dream.

南溪暮泛

迷花歸棹晚
待月下灘遲
醉裏猶垂釣
舟移夢不移

宋翼弼

SONG IK-P'IL　　1534–1599

# To the Moon

When on the wane, you are always impatient to wax,
But how so easily do you wane after waxing?
You are full only once in a month's thirty nights:
Man's mind in a lifetime is exactly the same.

望　月

未圓常恨就圓遲
圓後如何易就虧
三十夜中圓一夜
百年心事總如斯

宋翼弼

SONG IK-P'IL

# An Incidental Poem

I have lived in the mountains forty years,
Safe from involvement in the broils of the world.
I relax leisurely at my cottage in the spring breeze,
With smiling flowers and willows dozing.


偶 吟

四十年來臥碧山
是非何事到人間
小堂獨坐春風地
花笑柳眠閒又閒

成 渾

SŎNG HON    1535–1598

## On Resigning Office

Getting on depends not on man but on fate;
It is not my intention always to be on guard.
I have sent in my resignation, left the king,
And returned to the country, taking a small boat.
My dullness is only fit for tilling the soil,
Yet my dream vainly hovers around the palace.
Back at work in my thatched hut and stony fields,
I shall accept poverty in what remains of life.


求退有感

行藏由命豈由人
素志曾非在潔身
閶闔三章辭聖主
江湖一葦載孤臣
疎才只合耕南畝
清夢徒然繞北辰
茅屋石田還舊業
半生心事不憂貧

李　珥

YI I　1536–1584

# An Autumn Night

The rustling sound of falling leaves
I mistook for spattering rain.
I ordered a monk to go out and look;
He reports that the moon hangs on a bough.

秋　夜

蕭蕭落葉聲
錯認爲疎雨
呼僧出門看
月掛溪南樹

鄭　澈

CHŎNG CH'ŎL　　1536–1593

# Night at a Cottage

The moon fills the empty garden,
But where has the master gone?
Fallen leaves pile at the brushwood gate,
And wind-tossed pines murmur into night.

宿松江亭舍 (其三)

明月在空庭
主人何處去
落葉掩柴門
風松夜深語

鄭　澈

CHŎNG CH'ŎL

## Spring at Yongmun

As spring may come to my window at any time,
I roll up my screen early and let it down late.
Spring is at its peak at the mountain temple;
The monk on his way back passes the flowers, unaware.

龍門春望

日日軒窓似有期
開簾時早下簾遲
春光正在峰頭寺
花外歸僧自不知

白光勳

PAEK KWANG-HUN   1537–1582

## At Night on the Hansan Isle

Autumn light darkens over the sea;
Wild geese file high in the cold air.
As I toss about anxiously in the night
Moonlight catches my bow and sword.

閑山島夜吟

水國秋光暮
驚寒雁陣高
憂心輾轉夜
殘月照弓刀

李舜臣

YI SUN-SHIN    1545–1598

## Parting without a Word

A pretty girl, fifteen years old,
Was too shy to say a word to her lover.
Back home, she shuts up the double gate
And weeps before the moonlit pear-blossoms.

無語別

十五越溪女
羞人無語別
歸來掩重門
泣向梨花月

林　悌

IM CHE　　1549–1587

# Coming Home after a War

I couldn't bear the home-sickness,
So I sped my donkey a thousand leagues.
Spring is in its prime as of old,
But I find no man in the streets.
The storm has swept over the whole land,
Even the sun and moon are eclipsed.
All the prosperity that grew here has gone:
It is a chaos as at the world's dawn.


亂後歸故山

不堪鄉國戀
千里策蹇驢
節古春光滿
人消境落虛
山河風雨後
日月晦冥餘
剝盡繁華跡
渾如開闢初

張顯光

CHANG HYŎN-GWANG   1554–1637

# A Poor Woman

The poor woman, full of tears, rattled the shuttle,
Weaving material for her husband's winter clothes.
In the morning she cuts it down to pay the arrears,
One taxman leaves – and then another comes.

貧　女

貧女鳴梭淚滿腮
寒衣初擬爲郎裁
明朝裂與催租吏
一吏纔歸一吏來

柳夢寅

YU MONG-IN　　1559–1623

## A Lady's Complaint

I have soaked and stained my silk dress with tears;
Now I miss you the more as the grass greens again.
I have played a love-song on my jewelled lute:
The rain beats on the pear-blossom; I bolt the gate.

閨　　怨

錦帶羅裙積淚痕
一年芳草恨王孫
瑤箏彈盡江南曲
雨打梨花晝掩門

許楚姬

HŎ CH'O-HI　　1563–1589

# A Poor Girl

She is not an ugly girl;
She sews and weaves well.
Brought up in a poor family,
There's no match-maker she knows.

When she holds her scissors,
Her fingers are stiff with cold.
She makes wedding dresses for others:
She always sleeps alone.


## 貧女吟

豈是乏容色
工針復工織
少小長寒門
良媒不相識

手把金剪刀
夜寒十指直
爲人作嫁衣
年年還獨宿

許楚姬

HŎ CH'O-HI

## On a Monk's Poetry Scroll

Azaleas are blooming and swallows flying;
I wake up dazedly from a nap beside my lute.
A monk comes, but does not talk of the world,
Knowing I, too, want to live in the blue mountains.


次僧軸韻

躑躅花開亂燕飛
枯梧睡罷正忘機
僧來不作人間話
知我歸心在翠微

申　欽

SHIN HŬM　　1566–1628

## At the Grave of Chŏng Ch'ŏl

Leaves fall with rain in these vacant mountains;
Silent is the graceful voice of the poet-official.
Alas! I cannot offer you a cup this morning;
You had a song that foretold it, in the old days.

過松江墓

空山木落雨蕭蕭
相國風流此寂寥
惆悵一杯難更進
昔年歌曲即今朝

權 韠

KWŎN P'IL   1569–1612

# On an Autumn Night

The wild geese trail cold shrieks
And pass beyond the mountain walls.
I awake from a lonely dream of you;
My window is lit by the autumn moon.

秋夜有感

霜雁拖寒聲
寂寞過山城
思君孤夢罷
秋月照窗明

勝二喬

SŬNG I-KYO   *sixteenth century*

# An Incidental Poem

Flowers opened in the rain yesterday
And fell in the wind this morning.
What a pity that the season of spring
Should come and go in rain and wind!

偶 吟

花開昨日雨
花落今朝風
可憐一春事
往來風雨中

宋翰弼

SONG HAN-P'IL   *sixteenth century*

# On an Autumn Night

I wake from a dream, beneath a moonlit window;
Unable to control my longing, I sing alone in bed.
Now I regret that I thoughtlessly planted a tree:
Its rustling fills the garden with autumn grief.


秋夜作

小窓殘月夢初醒
一枕愁吟奈有情
却悔從前輕種樹
滿庭搖落作秋聲

金練光

KIM YŎN-GWANG   *sixteenth century*

# Waiting for a Lover

You promised to come, but you haven't:
The plum-blossoms in the garden begin to fall.
Suddenly I hear a magpie chirp on a bough,
And I have made up my face in vain.

閨　情

有約來何晚
庭梅欲謝時
忽聞枝上鵲
虛畫鏡中眉

李玉峰

YI OK-BONG　　*sixteenth century*

## Sorrows of Separation

Sorrows of separation have become a disease in me
That cannot be healed by wine, nor cured by medicine.
Under my quilt I weep, like water under the ice
Which flows day and night, but nobody knows.

離　恨

平生離恨成身病
酒不能療藥不治
衾裡泣如氷下水
日夜長流人不知

李玉峰

YI OK-BONG

# To a Lover

How are you getting along these days, my lord?
The moon shines at my window and I am sad.
Had I left footmarks where I came in dreams,
The stone path to your gate would have turned into sand.

贈雲江

近來安否問如何
月到紗窓妾恨多
若使夢魂行有跡
門前石路便成沙

李玉峰

YI OK-BONG

# At the Old Capital

The moonlit snow, colour of the former dynasty,
The cold bell, sound of the old country.
I stand pensively on the southern look-out;
Clouds rise, at dawn, above the castle ruins.

松都懷古

雪月前朝色
寒鍾故國聲
南樓愁獨立
殘郭曉雲生

權　韠

KWŎN KAP　　*sixteenth to seventeenth century*

# A New Swallow

Laughing away, with nonchalance, all human affairs,
I have closed my pine-twig gate in the spring rain.
But the newly returned swallow, outside the screen,
Seems to provoke me, arguing right and wrong.

詠新燕

萬事悠悠一笑揮
草堂春雨掩松扉
生憎簾外新歸燕
似向閒人説是非

李　植

YI SHIK　　1584–1647

## At My Study

My eyes fixed on the mountains and my ears on the lute,
How could affairs of the world ever disturb my mind?
Though nobody knows I am full of lively spirits,
Wildly I sing out a song, and then intone it alone.

樂書齊偶吟

眼在青山耳在琴
世間何事到吾心
滿腔浩氣無人識
一曲狂歌獨自唫

尹善道

YUN SŎN-DO   1587–1671

# To a Friend Retired in the Country

I hear you have settled back in the old county of Yangju,
Where you live in secret in the expanse of soft grass.
You may shun the sky under a big hat, astride on a cow,
Without turning toward Seoul even in the spring breeze.

寄東岳臺山別墅

聞君歸臥古楊州
細草長郊事事幽
大笠蔽天牛背穩
春風京洛不回頭

尹　暄

YUN HWŎN　　*sixteenth to seventeenth century*

# A Mountain Home

A poodle barks at the brushwood gate,
A white cloud wanders outside the window.
Who would come along such a stony path?
Only a bird warbles in the spring forest.

山　居

柴扉尨亂吠
窓外白雲迷
石徑人誰至
春林鳥自啼

許景胤

HŎ KYŎNG-YUN  *sixteenth to seventeenth century*

## On New Year's Eve

I drink till late at night, but cannot sleep;
The bell rings at dawn, but I am just the same.
Not that there is no new year's eve next year,
But it is only human to regret a year's departure.

除夜借高蜀州韻

酒盡殘燈也不眠
曉鍾鳴後轉依然
非關來歲無今夜
自是人情惜去年

姜栢年

KANG PAEK-NYŎN     1603–1681

## Going Up to the Capital

The green waters roar as if in anger,
As if frowning, the blue mountains hush.
Musing on the mountains and waters, I find
They hate my going into the wind and dust.


赴　京

綠水喧如怒
青山默似嚬
靜觀山水意
嫌我向風塵

宋時烈

SONG SHI-YŎL   1607–1689

# Elegy on Myself

I have never had a fill even of poor food,
So how could I hope for dishes and cups on my death?
I have never had more than a mugful of drink,
So how should I expect to taste a morsel of meat?
I go out of the gate of the capital city
To lie beneath the west hill in the field.
The wind in the forest sobs in sorrowful sounds;
The moon over the hills beams its sad light.
The world is a place for a short stay:
My real home is in the underworld.
Who knows if the joy of a skeleton
Will go on and on, like heaven and earth?


自 挽 (其二)

生不飽菽水
死何羅豆觴
一勺不復飲
一臠那得嘗
行出國都門
永野西陵傍
林風咽悲響
山月凝愁光

人間聊寄爾
九原眞我鄉
誰知髑髏樂
天地同未央

崔奇男

CH'OE KI-NAM   *seventeenth century*

# Sitting at Night

A quiet valley with no man's footprints,
An empty garden lit by the moon.
Suddenly my dog barks and I know
A friend with a bottle is knocking at the gate.

夜　　坐

谷靜無人跡
庭空有月痕
忽聞山犬吠
沽酒客歔門

嚴義吉

ŎM ŬI-GIL    *seventeenth century*

## A Lady's Complaint

The autumn wind withers the green leaves,
Tears wither the bloom of my face.
It's because of you that I have grown gaunt,
But you will cast me aside when you return.

閨　怨

金風凋碧葉
玉淚銷紅頰
瘦削只緣君
君歸應棄妾

曺臣俊

CHO SHIN-JUN　*seventeenth century*

Passing an Old Capital

Darkening clouds over ruined battlements,
Cold rain washes the desolate terrace.
The mountains are blue as of old,
But how many brave men have come and gone?

過古都

暮雲連廢堞
寒雨洗荒臺
山色青依舊
英雄幾去來

權大運

KWŎN TAE-UN     1633–1701

# In the Alley

She skimmed and fluttered in silk socks,
Went through a double gate and never reappeared.
But the snow is kind enough to remain in the alley,
Retaining her footprints in it beside the wall.


路上有見

凌波羅襪去翩翩
一入重門便杳然
惟有多情殘雪在
屐痕留印短墻邊

姜世晃

KANG SE-HWANG    1731–1799

## Looking into the Mirror on New Year's Day

Suddenly I discover more beard has grown,
Though it adds nothing to my six-foot height.
My face in the mirror changes as years go by,
But my heart remains as innocent as a year ago.

元朝對鏡

忽然添得數莖鬚
全不加長六尺軀
鏡裏容顔隨歲異
穉心猶自去年吾

朴趾源

PAK CHI-WŎN   1737–1805

# Parting from a Lover

My eyes, tearful, look at yours, tearful too;
My heart is breaking and so is your heart.
I have read, in books, of the sorrow of parting,
But never dreamed that it would happen to me.

奉別巡相李公

流淚眼看流淚眼
斷腸人對斷腸人
曾從卷裡尋常見
今日那知到妾身

桂 月

KYEWŎL  *eighteenth century*

# Lamenting Poverty

I set out to be happy with poverty,
But I find it difficult now I am poor.
I lose my dignity when my wife sighs,
And cannot be strict with the starving children.
Even trees and flowers look lifeless;
Poetry and books make no appeal.
The barley ripens by the hedge of the rich,
Good enough for the peasants to look at.


歎　貧

請事安貧語
貧來却未安
妻咨文采屈
兒餒教規寬
花木渾蕭颯
詩書摠汗漫
陶莊籬下麥
好付野人看

丁若鏞

CHŎNG YAK-YONG　　1762–1836

# Laughing by Myself

You may have grain, but nobody to eat it,
And worry about hunger, if you have sons.
When you're promoted, you must become a fool,
While the talented cannot find a place.
A household can seldom enjoy perfect bliss,
And the best principles always collapse.
A miserly father has always a prodigal son;
An intelligent wife a stupid husband.
When the moon is full, clouds often come;
When flowers bloom, the wind often blows.
This is the way of things.
So I laugh by myself, but nobody knows.

獨　　笑

有粟無人食
多男必患飢
達官必憃愚
才者無所施
家室少完福
至道常陵遲
翁嗇子每蕩
婦慧郎必癡
月滿頻值雲
花開風誤之
物物盡如此
獨笑無人知

丁若鏞

CHŎNG YAK-YONG

## A Dream

The way home is a thousand leagues;
An autumn night is even longer.
Ten times already I have been home,
But the cock has not yet crowed.

夜　夢

鄉路千里長
秋夜長於路
家山十徃來
簷鷄猶未啼

李亮淵

YI YANG-YŎN　1771–1853

# Written on a Cottage Wall

In a small cottage by a stumpy willow tree
A lonely couple live, both with white hair.
They have never gone beyond the path by the stream
For seventy years, with the corn in the ripening wind.

題村舍壁

禿柳一株屋數椽
翁婆白髮兩蕭然
未過三尺溪邊路
玉蜀西風七十年

金正喜

KIM CHŎNG-HI    1786–1856

# On Hearing, in Exile, of the Death of My Wife

Could I have Yüeh-lao appeal to the underworld
For us to change places in the next life,
I could make you feel the sorrow that I feel now,
When I die and you are alive a thousand leagues away.

配所輓妻喪

那將月姥訟冥司
來世夫妻易地爲
我死君生千里外
使君知我此心悲

金正喜

KIM CHŎNG-HI

# Ch'usŏk

The widow, on the day of Ch'usŏk,
Wails all day at her husband's grave.
In the field below, the rice is ripening
Which they tended together, but now cannot share.

秋　夕

寡婦當秋夕
青山盡日哭
下有黃稻熟
同耕不同食

鄭象覿

CHŎNG SANG-GWAN  *eighteenth to nineteenth century*

## On the Roadside Monument

Funds were extorted for the old magistrate's monument,
But who exploited the people and forced them away?
The piece of stone is speechless at the roadside:
How can the new magistrate compare with the old?

題路傍去思碑

去思橫欲刻碑錢
編戶流亡孰使然
片石無言當路立
新官何似舊官賢

李尚迪

YI SANG-JŎK   1804–1865

# At an Inn

Equipped with only a stick on a thousand-league journey,
I have seven pennies left; I say it's still a lot.
I tell these coins to remain deep, deep in my pocket,
But what shall I do at an inn when the sun goes down?

艱飲野店

千里行裝付一柯
餘錢七葉尚云多
囊中戒爾深深在
野店斜陽見酒何

金炳淵

KIM PYŎNG-YŎN    1807–1857

## To an Ungenerous Host

A bowl of gruel on the four-legged pine table
Reflects the sunlight and the wandering clouds.
Don't tell me, Sir, that you are ashamed of yourself:
I love to see the mountains come imaged in water.

無 題

四脚松盤粥一器
天光雲影共徘徊
主人莫道無顔色
吾愛青山倒水來

金炳淵

KIM PYŎNG-YŎN

## On My Way to Such'un

Down below, the river reflects the sky and greenery;
I drop my walking stick and fall asleep in the grass.
Alas! I am poorer than the willows on the long river-bank,
Still in my cotton-padded garb, though the spring wind
    has gone.

暮春途中

襪底江光綠浸天
昭陽芳草放筇眠
浮生不及長堤柳
過盡東風未脫綿

姜瑋

KANG WI    1820–1884

# Lodging in the Capital

On my way to the capital at sundown,
Knotweeds blossom white in the autumn wind.
When I get drunk, I fall asleep at any house:
So, why do I need to ask whose?

宿松京

落日松京道
秋風白蓼花
醉來仍着睡
何必問誰家

李種元

YI CHONG-WŎN    1849–?

# The East Lake

The spring water of the east lake is deep, deep blue;
White birds stand out on it by twos and threes.
When they have flown away at the soft sound of an oar,
The lake is filled with mountains in the evening sun.

東　湖

東湖春水碧於藍
白鳥分明見兩三
柔櫓一聲飛去盡
夕陽山色滿空潭

鄭　鳳

CHŎNG PONG　　*nineteenth century*

# The Swing

The girl, fourteen years old but bigger than me,
Has learned to swing like a swallow flying.
As I dare not speak aloud from outside her window,
I scribble on a persimmon leaf and throw it to her.

鞦　韆

小姑十四大於余
學得鞦韆飛燕如
隔窓不敢高聲語
柿葉題投數字書

黃　五

HWANG O　　*nineteenth century*

# Waiting for a Lover

He swore he would come at moonrise;
The moon has risen, but he doesn't come.
Probably where he lives, the mountains
Are high and the moon is slow to rise.

待郎君

郎云月出來
月出郎不來
想應君在處
山高月上遲

凌　雲

NŬNGUN　　*nineteenth century*

## In a Boat

Flowers were opening at the house where I spent the night;
This morning I cross a river afloat with petals.
Spring is busy like people, coming and going:
No sooner have I seen the flowers than I see them fall.

舟　中

昨宿開花山下家
今朝又涉落花波
春光却似人來去
纔見開花又落花

交河落花津女

ANONYMOUS WOMAN　　*nineteenth century*

# Peach Blossom

In rain it opens, and falls in wind.
How many days can we see the peach blossom?
This brevity is in the blossom's nature:
Not that the wind has been guilty, or the rain kind.

桃　花

開時有雨落時風
看得桃花幾日紅
自是桃花身上事
風曾何罪雨何功

李　沂

YI KI    *nineteenth century*

## On a Great-Granddaughter's Death

Sick for seven years in a life of eight,
You must indeed be restful, being dead.
But how sad it is that in tonight's snow
You part from your mother without feeling cold!

悼孫女殤兒

八歲七年病
歸臥爾應安
只憐今夜雪
離母不知寒

南　氏

ANONYMOUS WOMAN  *date unknown*

# Autumn Rain at a Remote Temple

The rain drizzles on Mount Diamond in September;
Every leaf drips with the sound of autumn.
I have shed silent tears alone for ten years,
Wetting my miserable cowl, but in vain.

雨聲孤寺秋

九月金剛蕭瑟雨
雨中無葉不鳴秋
十年獨下無聲淚
淚濕袈衣空自愁

女僧慧定

HYEJŎNG    *date unknown*

# Hearing of a Disaster

Though River Han is hushed and Mount Pugak frowns,
High officials still swarm about the world.
Look at the lives of traitors in bygone times;
No one who sells the pass ever gets killed.

聞　變

洌水吞聲白岳嚬
紅塵依舊簇簪紳
請看歷代奸臣傳
賣國元無死國人

　黃　玹

HWANG HYŎN　1855–1910

# On Killing Myself

Growing old through all these turbulent years,
I have often come very close to ending my life.
But today truly I have no other choice:
A flaring candle lights up the dark, blue sky.

絕命詩

亂離滾到白頭年
幾合捐生却未然
今日眞成無可奈
輝輝風燭照蒼天

黃　玹

HWANG HYŎN

# Notes

*page*

26  Mount Kaya is located in South Kyongsang Province. Towards the end of the Silla Dynasty, the poet retired, in his later years, to the mountain with its torrential gorge.

27  Ch'oe Kwang-yu was a contemporary of Ch'oe Ch'i-wǒn, and like him studied in Chang-an, the capital city of the T'ang dynasty.

28  The location of the Cold Pine Pavilion and the Mirror Lake is Kangnŭng, a city on the east coast of Korea. The poem is said to be a translated version of a Korean-language song.

29  The Taedong River flows through P'yŏngyang.

30  The Kamno-sa Temple was located in Kaesŏng, about 40 miles north of Seoul.

31  Kŭmyang-hyŏn is now the Kŭmhwa area of Kangwŏn Province.

32  There is a bird called in Chinese 'carrying a bottle'.

33  The Hsiao-hsiang, a river in southern China, was famous for its scenery. The poem was written on a picture drawn by a Sung painter.

34  Nakchu is now Sangju in North Kyŏngsang Province.

37  The Nakdong River flows south through North and South Kyŏngsang Provinces. 'As red as a monkey's blood' is an idiom in Chinese.

38  This poem, formerly attributed to Ch'oe Ch'ung (984-1068), has recently been identified as being by Ch'oe Hang.

42  Wŏngam was a monk.

53  Sŏng Sam-mun was one of the six courtiers of King Tanjong who, when the king had been forced, by his uncle Sejo, to abdicate his throne, attempted his restoration. The attempt was detected and they subsequently were executed.

54  In the Far East, the west wind is the autumn wind.

57  Tanjong, the sixth king of the Yi Dynasty, succeeded to the throne at the age of twelve, but was made to abdicate after three years' reign and forced to kill himself in his exile. In this poem, he finds his own likeness in a nightingale. Line 6 may be taken as a symbolic expression of the quality of the nightingale's song and also a reference to the cruelties which ensued from his abdication.

68  'Plum blossoms' here is the name of a Chinese tune for the flute.

76  Yongmun is the name of a place not very far from Seoul.
77  Yi Sun-shin is the famous Korean admiral who defeated the Japanese navy during the Japanese invasion of Korea towards the end of the sixteenth century. His naval base was situated at the Hansan Isle.
84  Chŏng Ch'ŏl (1538-1593), a great poet and high official, has a Korean-language song, 'Offering a Cup'.
88  In Korea, a magpie is said to herald a welcome guest.
94  Yangju is a county east of Seoul.
98  It is a Confucian custom to offer food and wine to the dead.
109  Yüeh-lao is the Chinese marriage-goddess.
110  Ch'usŏk is the traditional day in autumn when offerings are made at the graves of one's family members.
113  This poem is said to have been occasioned by a humiliating meal a country squire gave to the poet in the yard of his house.
114  Such'un is now Ch'unch'ŏn of Kangwŏn Province. The last line alludes to the fact that the spring wind has blown away the cotton-like catkins of the willows and changed the trees into spring attire.
121  Only the poet's surname, Nam, is known.
122  Mount Diamond, famous for its scenic beauty, is situated on the east coast of Korea, just north of the present demilitarized zone. Hyejŏng was a Buddhist nun.
123  River Han and Mount Pugak are both located in Seoul. This poem was written when the poet heard of the treaty signed between Korea and Japan in 1905, by which Korea was made a Japanese protectorate.
124  This is one of four poems the poet wrote on his suicide in protest against Japan's annexation of Korea in 1910.

## POETICA

1. THE POEMS OF MELEAGER
   Peter Whigham and Peter Jay

2. THE NOISE MADE BY POEMS
   Peter Levi

3. THE SATIRES OF PERSIUS
   W.S. Merwin, introduced by William S. Anderson

4. FLOWER AND SONG (Aztec Poems)
   Edward Kissam and Michael Schmidt

5. PALLADAS: POEMS
   Tony Harrison

6. THE SONG OF SONGS
   Peter Jay and David Goldstein
   illustrated by Nikos Stavroulakis

7. D.G. ROSSETTI: THE EARLY ITALIAN POETS
   Sally Purcell, preface by John Wain

8. PETRARCH: SONGS AND SONNETS FROM LAURA'S LIFETIME
   Nicholas Kilmer

9. VASKO POPA: THE GOLDEN APPLE
   Andrew Harvey and Anne Pennington

10. VICTOR HUGO: THE DISTANCE, THE SHADOWS
    Harry Guest

11. OLD ENGLISH RIDDLES
    Michael Alexander

12. AN UNOFFICIAL RILKE
    Michael Hamburger

13. GOETHE: POEMS AND EPIGRAMS
    Michael Hamburger

14. MARTIAL: LETTER TO JUVENAL
    Peter Whigham, introduced by J.P. Sullivan

15. LI HE: GODDESSES, GHOSTS, AND DEMONS
    J.D. Frodsham

16. NIETZSCHE: DITHYRAMBS OF DIONYSUS
    R.J. Hollingdale

17. POEMS OF JULES LAFORGUE
    Peter Dale

18. GÉRARD DE NERVAL: THE CHIMERAS
    Peter Jay and Richard Holmes

19. THE LAMENTATION OF THE DEAD
    Peter Levi

20. APOLLINAIRE: SELECTED POEMS
    Oliver Bernard

*also published by Anvil in the Poetica series*

# GODDESSES, GHOSTS, AND DEMONS
## The Collected Poems of Li He (790-816)
*translated and introduced by J.D. Frodsham*

Among the great T'ang writers and philosophers, Li He ('the ghost') stood apart as a poet of remarkable and eccentric genius. As mystic and shaman-poet, he writes of goddesses, of the supernatural and demonic, of time and of alchemy. Taoist and Buddhist, his verse is distinguished by a wild, exotic pessimism and a romantic extravagance which make him seem unsettlingly modern.

J.D. Frodsham's magnificent translation of the 240 poems is accompanied by an outstanding introduction on Li He's poetry and his position among his contemporaries. He has also provided extensive notes on the poems.

*USA edition: North Point Press*